A Palm Sunday Ex

Hosanna to You, Jesus!

Story by Marisa Mignolli
Translated and adapted by Anne Joan Flanagan, FSP
Illustrated by M. Luisa Benigni

Pauline
ST. PAUL BOOKS & MEDIA

St. Paul Book & Media Centers

ALASKA
750 West 5th Ave., Anchorage, AK 99501; 907-272-8183
CALIFORNIA
3908 Sepulveda Blvd., Culver City, CA 90230; 310-397-8676
5945 Balboa Ave., San Diego, CA 92111; 619-565-9181
46 Geary Street, San Francisco, CA 94108; 415-781-5180
FLORIDA
145 S.W. 107th Ave., Miami, FL 33174; 305-559-6715
HAWAII
1143 Bishop Street, Honolulu, HI 96813; 808-521-2731
ILLINOIS
172 North Michigan Ave., Chicago, IL 60601; 312-346-4228
LOUISIANA
4403 Veterans Memorial Blvd., Metairie, LA 70006; 504-887-7631
MASSACHUSETTS
50 St. Paul's Ave., Jamaica Plain, Boston, MA 02130; 617-522-8911
Rte. 1, 885 Providence Hwy., Dedham, MA 02026; 617-326-5385
MISSOURI
9804 Watson Rd., St. Louis, MO 63126; 314-965-3512
NEW JERSEY
561 U.S. Route 1, Wick Plaza, Edison, NJ 08817; 908-572-1200
NEW YORK
150 East 52nd Street, New York, NY 10022; 212-754-1110
78 Fort Place, Staten Island, NY 10301; 718-447-5071
OHIO
2105 Ontario Street (at Prospect Ave.), Cleveland, OH 44115; 216-621-9427
PENNSYLVANIA
510 Holstein Street, Bridgeport, PA 19405; 215-277-7728
SOUTH CAROLINA
243 King Street, Charleston, SC 29401; 803-577-0175
TENNESSEE
4811 Poplar Ave., Memphis, TN 38117 901-761-2987
TEXAS
114 Main Plaza, San Antonio, TX 78205; 210-224-8101
VIRGINIA
1025 King Street, Alexandria, VA 22314; 703-549-3806
GUAM
285 Farenholt Avenue, Suite 308, Tamuning, Guam 96911; 671-646-7745
CANADA
3022 Dufferin Street, Toronto, Ontario, Canada M6B 3T5; 416-781-9131

Original title: *Osanna a Te Gesú: Con Gesú verso Gerusalemme*

Translated from the Italian and adapted by Anne Joan Flanagan, FSP

Published by Pauline Books & Media, 50 St. Paul's Avenue, Boston, MA 02130

Pauline Books & Media is the publishing house of the Daughters of St. Paul, an international congregation of women religious serving the Church with the communications media.

2 3 4 5 6 7 8 9 99 98 97 96 95 94

INTRODUCTION

How can we speak to children of Jesus' Paschal Mystery? How can we help them feel present for this foundational event of Christian faith?

Hosanna to You, Jesus! creates a "real-life" setting for the children to adapt imaginatively to themselves. They meet Daniel and his sturdy donkey, Balaam. Jesus has asked to ride Balaam into Jerusalem.

With the excuse of not abandoning his donkey, Daniel follows Jesus up to Jerusalem and discovers why the crowd so joyfully proclaims him "Lord."

It was a day of
sun and warmth.
Spring
was here!

Daniel and his friend Sara
danced in the pure light.
But Balaam, the donkey, was not
so cheerful. He stomped
on the rope that kept him tied up.

Suddenly, two shadows
appeared on the wall.
Balaam protested: Hee-haw, hee-haw.

Daniel's father
came out to see what was wrong.

Two strangers were untying Balaam!

"What are you doing?"
Daniel's father demanded.
"Why have you untied the donkey?"
"The Lord has need of him,"
answered one of the strangers.
"The donkey will be returned to you,"
the other reassured.
Surprised, Daniel's father let them
lead the animal down
the road to Jerusalem.

"Papa, who is this 'Lord'?"
Daniel wanted to know.
"And why does he want our donkey?"
"Perhaps it is for someone to go to the city
for Passover, to thank God
for saving our people from slavery
in Egypt," his father replied.

But Daniel had
already run toward
the road the strangers had taken.
"Balaam! Balaam!"
Daniel shouted,
"Wait for me! I'm coming, too!"

Daniel came to a dip in the road,
and there was his donkey—surrounded
by people. "Balaam, here I am!"
the boy shouted breathlessly.

Balaam nuzzled Daniel's cheek.
A gentle man looked on, smiling.
And Daniel knew:
this must be the Lord!
"I am Daniel," he said to the Lord.
"And my name is Jesus."
"You can use my donkey if you need him,"
Daniel said.

Someone laid a red cloak on Balaam's
back and Jesus mounted.
At first, the animal seemed unsteady.
No one had ever ridden him before.

The crowd moved aside
and a little parade started.
People lined the road, laying cloaks
and branches on the path.

Some cried out:
"Hosanna! Hosanna!"
Others responded:
"Blessed is he who comes in the name of the Lord!"

"Hosanna!"

Daniel cried
with delight.

At the city gates, the parade stopped.
Children gathered around Jesus,
trying to out-shout each other:
"Long live Jesus! Long live the King of peace!"

A voice
from the crowd asked,
"Who is this man?"
The crowd answered,
"It is the prophet Jesus,
from Nazareth."
"A prophet? What has he done?"

A woman spoke up.
"I am a widow from Naim.
My only son was dead,
but Jesus brought him back to life."

"I was a leper," a man said bravely. "Jesus made me well."

Daniel listened with amazement to what the people were saying about Jesus.
"Now I understand why they call Jesus the Lord.
He has done only good.
Long live the Lord Jesus!"

There was happy shouting everywhere. Only Jesus was quiet. Jesus dismounted and lightly touched the donkey's muzzle. Then Jesus looked at Daniel for a long time.

Daniel watched as Jesus turned to enter the Temple alone.

"Come, Balaam," Daniel said.

"Now you are the most important donkey in the whole world!

You have served Jesus, the one who cures the blind and the lepers,
who raises the dead and who...
looked right at us."

"Let's go tell everyone about him.
And then we can come back to
Jerusalem soon, to see him again."

SHARING DANIEL'S ADVENTURE

Projects and Prayers for Home and Classroom

REFLECTION

With Daniel, we meet Jesus.

Daniel's adventure started at his own house. He heard about Jesus for the first time from two strangers who came to borrow the donkey. Wanting to know more, Daniel followed them, leaving his games and his friends behind and going on the way in search of Jesus. His desire was rewarded: Daniel met Jesus. Daniel was happy to be with Jesus, and he followed him. Along the road up to Jerusalem, Daniel joined in the happy praise the crowd sang to Jesus.

At the city gates, someone called out, "Who is this?"

Deep in his heart, Daniel asked the same question. Daniel wanted to know Jesus better.

Thanks to the witness of others, Daniel's heart opened to Jesus and to his gifts of faith and love. Daniel understood that Jesus was his best friend, and that Jesus wanted Daniel to follow him.

❑ Invite each child to express his/her favorite part of Daniel's story and to describe in words or with a drawing what it would have been like if they were in Daniel's place.

❑ Invite the children to describe Daniel before he met Jesus. Was Daniel changed by his meeting with Jesus?

❑ Go back to page 24, where Daniel watches Jesus enter the Temple by himself. Ask the children: What is going to happen to Jesus? (The events of holy week: Jesus will soon be handed over to enemies, arrested, hit and made fun of, put to death—and raised from the dead.)

❑ Imagine if Daniel had met Jesus on Easter. What would he have said? How might Jesus have replied?

❑ Let the children visualize Daniel and Balaam's return home. What did Daniel have to talk about? Let the children choose different persons in Daniel's neighborhood (father, mother, Sara, neighbor) and say what Daniel might have told those persons.

❑ Prepare a large poster with a road running through rolling hills, culminating in a cross and the words: *Jesus Goes to Jerusalem.* The children can take turns drawing their own favorite scene along the road.

CELEBRATION

The purpose of this prayer-celebration is to foster in the children an appreciation for the profound links which unite as one event all that happened in the last days of Jesus' earthly life.

Jesus' entrance into Jerusalem, the Last Supper, the plottings of his enemies, his condemnation by Pilate, the abandonment of the disciples, the crucifixion, death, burial and resurrection: these are the "stages" in the one event we call the Paschal Mystery.

The Church helps us enter gradually into this mystery through the liturgies of Holy Week, culminating in the Easter Triduum: from the Evening Mass of the Lord's Supper on Thursday through the Easter Vigil.

In today's prayer-celebration, we recall these different events "in sign" in order to discover at last that all are born of the word which Jesus has proclaimed and fully lived: "This is my commandment, that you love one another as I have loved you. No one has greater love than this, to lay down one's life for one's friends" (Jn 15:12-13; NRSV).

I. The Way

The celebration begins with a procession led by the "Jesus enters Jerusalem" poster (if one was made as part of the follow-up to the story). The children themselves carry in the things needed for the celebration. Those who have no items to carry may hold palm branches or flowers. The leader should process in the midst of the children.

Half way through, pause to hear the proclamation of Jesus' messianic entry into Jerusalem (Lk 19:28-40).

II. The Table

The procession continues until all are around the table that was set up earlier. The children now prepare the table:

—covering it with a tablecloth,

—spreading a cloth napkin,

—setting on the napkin a torn loaf of pita bread,

—placing a cup or chalice near the bread,

—and decorating the table with the branches and flowers they carried.

As the children proceed to the chairs or pews, a lector proclaims Luke's account of the institution of the Eucharist (Lk 22:14-15; 19-20). The children may respond with a simple, sung acclamation.

III. The Cross

A small group (cross-bearer and two or four companions) may process to the front. The cross-bearer holds the crucifix before the assembly, while the children take turns reading Christ's last words from previously prepared strips of paper distributed earlier. The papers can then be fastened to the arms of the cross. (Very small children can simply repeat the phrases proclaimed by the leader.)

IV. Silence

Gradually dim the lights until only the crucifix is illuminated. Invite the children to quiet prayer. After 30-60 seconds, play soft music and proclaim the account of the death of Jesus (Lk 23:44-46).

V. The New Day

Prepare the assembly for the announcement of resurrection by giving each one an unlit candle. Call them to stand up, while lively music begins to play. Turn on the lights with a cry of "Alleluia" which all may repeat.

Have a student carry a large white candle to a place of honor (preferably near the cross). Light it (or pin a paper "flame" in place) and invite the children to come in turn to light their candles with pre-made paper flames. Throughout this rite, the Alleluia may be sung.

When all candles are "lit," proclaim the resurrection of Jesus (Jn 20:1-9). Let all join the hymn of the angels: Holy, Holy, Holy! Conclude with a dismissal, such as: Christ is Risen. Let us go in peace, Alleluia!